Survivor's Science in the

Forest

Peter D. Riley

HODDER
Wayland

An imprint of Hodder Children's Books

© 2004 White-Thomson Publishing Ltd

White-Thomson Publishing Ltd,
2-3 St Andrew's Place, Lewes,
East Sussex BN7 1UP

Published in Great Britain in 2004 by Hodder
Wayland, an imprint of Hodder Children's
Books

This book was produced for White-Thomson
Publishing Ltd by Ruth Nason.

Design and illustration: Carole Binding

British Library Cataloguing in Publication Data
Riley, Peter D.
    In the Forest. - (Survivor's Science)
    1. Forest ecology - Juvenile literature
    I. Title
    577.3
ISBN 0 7502 4240 X

Printed in Hong Kong by Wing King Tong

Hodder Children's Books
A division of Hodder Headline Limited
338 Euston Road, London NW1 3BH

Acknowledgements
The author and publishers thank the following for their permission to
reproduce photographs: Carole Binding: cover centre and pages 14, 17t, 20t,
21t, 22t, 39; Corbis: pages 1 and 10 (Wolfgang Kaehler), 4 (Robert Holmes), 6
and 37 (Wolfgang Kaehler), 11 (Paul A. Souders), 16 (Eric and David Hosking),
24 (Nik Wheeler), 27 (Roman Soumar), 31 (Layne Kennedy), 32 (Paul A.
Souders), 33 (James Marshall), 34 (Darrell Gulin), 35 (Layne Kennedy), 38 (Phil
Schermeister), 44 (Pat O'Hara); Ecoscene: pages 7 and 40r (Alan Towse), 19
(Andrew Brown); Science Photo Library: pages 17b (Dr Jeremy Burgess), 22b
(Stephen Kraseman); Still Pictures: pages 8 (T. de Salis), 20b (Anthony Leclerc),
30 and cover (Fred Pearce), 40l (Kevin Schafer), 42 (Lynn Rogers). The science
activity photographs are by Carole Binding.

Contents

Introduction

A wood can be an exciting place, with shady places to hide, noisy birds in the trees and the chance to see deer and squirrels. Woods are groups of trees, possibly covering a hillside or growing along a riverbank for a kilometre or so. Forests are like woods but they are enormous. They cover mountainsides, sometimes for thousands of square kilometres. We are going to look at woods and forests in the Northern and Southern Hemispheres of the Earth, in the **temperate** and cooler regions rather than in **tropical** areas. Some are made up of **conifers**, others of **broad-leaved trees**. You may also know of a wood or forest with both kinds of tree.

The keys to survival

It is thought that the first people lived in woods and forests. They survived because they could find food and use the materials around them in many ways. They made tools from stone, wood and antlers. Later on, people learned to farm crops and animals. These needed space, and many woods and forests were destroyed to make fields.

Today few people live in woods and forests, but many go to camp and trek through the trees. Scientists may go there to study plants and animals, or the soils or weather conditions in which the trees grow. People who want to go exploring remote parts of the world often start by camping in a wood. They learn survival skills, just as ancient peoples did. Perhaps you have already done this and taken your first steps in becoming a real explorer.

Discovering with science

For thousands of years people have investigated their surroundings and made discoveries that have helped them survive. About 400 years ago, a way of investigating called the scientific method was devised, to help us understand our world more clearly. The main features of the scientific method are:

1 Making an **observation**

2 Thinking of an idea to explain the observation

3 Doing a test or experiment to test the idea

4 Looking at the result of the test and comparing it with the idea

Today the scientific method is used to provide explanations for almost everything. In this book you can find out about the science that helps people, plants and animals survive in woods and forests. You can also try some activities to see how different areas of science, such as the study of materials, forces and the weather, help us understand how people can survive among the trees. In these activities you may use the whole of the scientific method or just parts of it, such as making observations or doing experiments. But you will always be using science to make discoveries.

Are you ready to find out how people can survive in woods and forests? Turn the page to find the main forest regions.

Make a barometer to investigate air pressure.
Page 15

Find out if pine cones can predict rain.
Page 18

Test how winged fruits spin in the air.
Page 21

Observe plant growth.
Page 23

Test natural material for insulation.
Page 26

Investigate forces on a tent peg.
Page 29

Test the effect of water on food.
Page 36

Find out how birds perch on trees.
Page 41

Learn to tie an important knot.
Page 43

Send messages using sound.
Page 45

Forest regions

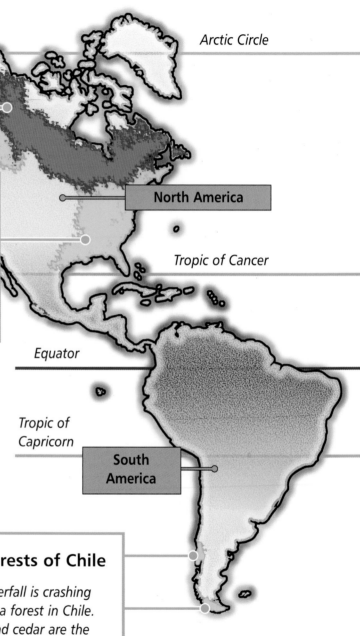

The boreal forest

The lodge pole pine, Sitka spruce and balsam fir are some of the many kinds of conifers here. Animals include moose, elk, brown bears and great-horned owls. The Athapaskan people lived here for over 2,000 years, hunting and fishing.

The broad-leaved forests of the Eastern United States

Oak, hickory and maple are some of the many trees here. White-tailed deer, black bears and red-headed woodpeckers live in the forests. The forests were home to the Iroquois and other Native American peoples.

The largest forest in the world is made by conifers, which grow close to the Arctic region, all the way around the globe. Broad-leaved forests are found in many other places. In the past these forests were much larger, but they have been cleared away so that people can set up farms, towns and cities.

Arctic Circle

North America

Tropic of Cancer

Equator

Tropic of Capricorn

South America

The forests of Chile

This waterfall is crashing through a forest in Chile. Beech and cedar are the main trees in the forests of southern Chile, while monkey puzzle trees form woodlands.

 Cold forest regions

 Temperate forest regions

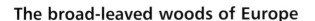

The broad-leaved woods of Europe

Oak, ash and beech are common woodland trees. Foxes, roe-deer and sparrow-hawks make their home here. In the past the woodlands formed vast forests which were home to Stone Age people including the **Neanderthals**.

The taiga

'Taiga' is Russian for barren land: compared to the thick forests further south, it appears that few plants grow well here. The main tree is the larch, though many other conifers grow with it. Animals include brown bears and elk. The Sami people of Northern Europe and the Evenk of Russia live in the taiga and herd reindeer.

Asia

Europe

The forests of Szechwan

Coniferous *forests and broad-leaved forests grow in this region of mountains in China. Rhododendrons and bamboo grow here. The forests are home to the giant panda and the ring-necked pheasant.*

The forests of New Zealand

On the North Island, kauri trees reach a height of 40 metres. Conditions on the South Island are too cold for the kauri, and forests here contain matai and miro trees, reaching a height of 25 metres. The kiwi is a flightless bird living in these forests.

Africa

Australia

The forests of South Eastern Australia

Over 500 kinds of eucalyptus trees grow in Australia and, where weather conditions allow, they can make forests. One type of forest eucalyptus is the blue gum. Some forests are home to the koala, which feeds on eucalyptus leaves. In the past, Aborigine people lived in the forests.

The forests of Tasmania

Nineteen kinds of eucalyptus trees, including the Smithton peppermint, grow in Tasmania. There is also a kind of beech tree called the tanglefoot. Animals here include the Tasmanian devil (a carnivorous **marsupial**, *which looks like a small black bear) and egg-laying mammals such as the platypus and the echidna. Aborigine people living on the coast used forest materials to help them survive.*

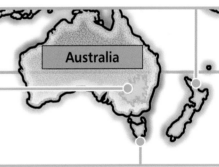

How are trees and bushes different from other plants?

Trees and bushes are found almost everywhere, even in city streets. As they are so common, people tend to ignore them. Some people even think that trees and bushes are not plants but something different. In fact, they are just plants with woody stems and roots.

Most plants grow shoots in the springtime. The shoot grows leaves and flowers. The flowers make seeds and release them. Then the shoot dies and the plant remains alive as a root or a bulb in the soil. The plants do this in order to survive the winter. Their flimsy stems could not stand up to the strong winter winds and the freezing temperatures. Plants that grow and die back in this way are known as **herbaceous** plants. Many kinds grow in woods and forests, between the trees.

Trees and bushes have developed a way to survive the harsh winter conditions above ground. This allows them to grow large and to produce huge numbers of seeds. By producing large numbers of seeds, the trees increase the chance that some seeds will survive and grow into new trees to replace old trees which die.

▲ Bluebells are a herbaceous plant. They grow each spring and then die back again.

How wood helps the tree survive

The wood of a tree helps it survive in several ways. Part of the wood is made of strong **fibres**, which join firmly together to make the trunk strong and flexible. This allows the tree to sway in the wind without breaking.

Plants need to get water to all parts of their bodies and so there are rings of water-carrying tubes in a tree's wood. A tree produces a new ring of tubes, around the outside of the existing rings, every year. The new ring is larger than the one made the year before, to provide enough water for the new parts of the tree that have grown.

As the tree grows older, it stores some of the food it has made in the rings nearer the centre. The tree can draw on this food store through the winter, to keep itself alive when the leaves cannot make food.

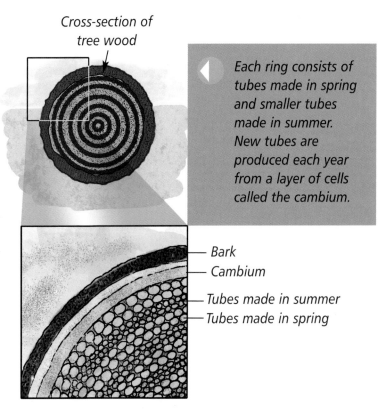

Cross-section of tree wood

Each ring consists of tubes made in spring and smaller tubes made in summer. New tubes are produced each year from a layer of cells called the cambium.

— Bark
— Cambium
— Tubes made in summer
— Tubes made in spring

How do trees make food?

Like almost all plants, trees make food in their leaves. The leaves contain a green substance called **chlorophyll**. It traps some of the sunlight that shines on the leaf. Sunlight is a form of energy and, in the leaf, some of this energy is used to make food, while the rest is stored in the food that is made. The food may then be moved to other parts of the tree where twigs and roots are growing, or stored in the wood for later use in winter.

How bark helps the tree survive

The outer part of the wood is covered in bark. This forms an **insulating** blanket around all parts of the trunk, branches and twigs. This means that it stops heat escaping from inside the tree, so that the tree does not become so cold that it would freeze and die.

Just under the bark are tubes that carry food from the leaves to all parts of the tree. If the bark is cut, these tubes are damaged and the tree may suffer because food cannot move. Without food, root tips do not grow through the soil, and seeds and fruits do not form on the twigs.

Wood is a living material and almost all living things need **oxygen**. The bark has holes in it, called lenticels, which let oxygen pass through to keep the wood alive.

Weather in forest regions

Coniferous forests grow in cold regions, like the Russian taiga.

If you are going to explore a forest region, you need to know what weather to expect, so that you can take clothes to match the weather conditions.

In the **boreal** and coniferous forests there are short, cool summers and long, very cold winters, so warm clothes are needed all year round. In broad-leaved forests, the weather conditions can vary from day to day and even from hour to hour. If people don't have clothes to match all the changing weather conditions, they could be in danger.

The weather changes are caused by the way the air moves over the surface of the Earth.

Air masses

Sometimes the air moves quickly and winds are created. At other times the air may move very slowly or even stay still. When air stays in one place for a long time, it takes up some of the features of its surroundings. For example, think about opening a fridge, first thing in the morning. The air that has been trapped inside all night feels very cold. Or think how, after someone has had a long hot bath, the air in the bathroom is warm and moist. In a similar way, when large amounts of air called 'air masses' stay still over a region of the Earth, they cool down or warm up, depending on where they are resting.

Warm air masses form near the equator, and cold air masses form in the polar regions. However, air masses do not stay in one place for very long and eventually they move away. There are boundaries between the warm and cold air masses of the world, as the map shows, but the boundaries move up and down the globe as the different air masses push on each other.

Cold air masses

Warm air masses

Cold air masses

▲ The dotted lines show the boundaries where the cold air masses and warm air masses push on each other.

When different air masses meet, they produce changeable weather. This often means that it rains at any time of year. This is just the kind of weather that broad-leaved trees need, and this is why broad-leaved forests grow in regions where the air masses meet.

▼ Hikers in the broad-leaved forests need to be prepared for sudden rain.

Warm and cold fronts

A front forms where two air masses meet and travel in the same direction. Trekkers can learn to recognize types of clouds that mean a front is coming, and use them to predict the weather.

If a warm air mass catches up with a cold air mass, the warm air rises gradually over the cold air and a warm front is formed. As the warm air rises, **water vapour** in the air **condenses** and forms clouds. They build up in an orderly way into certain types. This tells you that a warm front is approaching. A warm front produces long periods of heavy rain. When you see it coming, you can put on waterproof clothing, and you may decide to make a camp until it has passed.

If a cold air mass catches up with a warm air mass, the cold air pushes its way under the warm air. This makes the warm air rise quickly and creates winds that move upwards. The water vapour in the warm air condenses and the wind blows it into thick, tall storm clouds, called cumulonimbus. These clouds produce short

Cumulonimbus clouds can rise many kilometres into the air. They may be followed by smaller shower clouds.

A warm front and its cloud types

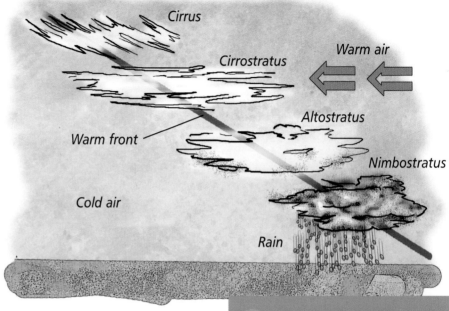

Cirrus

Cirrostratus

Warm air

Altostratus

Warm front

Nimbostratus

Cold air

Rain

Cirrus clouds are like huge feathers, while the different kinds of stratus clouds form layers at different heights above the ground.

A cold front and its cloud types

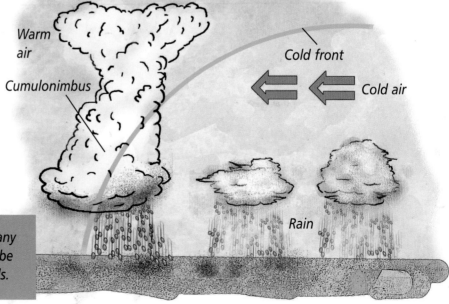

Warm air

Cold front

Cumulonimbus

Cold air

Rain

showers of very heavy rain and sometimes hail. When you see the clouds of a cold front approaching, you can put on your waterproof clothing and perhaps find somewhere to shelter. But after a short time it may be fine again for you to continue your journey.

Air pressure

There is another way to use the air to predict the weather. This is by using a **barometer** (see pages 14-15) to detect changes in air pressure.

The air is made up of particles of gases, such as oxygen and nitrogen. They push on everything around them and this push is called air pressure. The way air pressure changes is very complicated, but one cause of it changing is when a front forms and air rises. The particles of gases in the rising air cannot push as strongly on the ground below them. We say that the air pressure falls and becomes low.

Air pressure also changes when warm air cools. As the warm air cools, the particles of gases come closer together. Cool air sinks towards the Earth's surface and piles up there, bringing a large number of particles together to push on everything around them. We say that the air pressure has risen and become high.

When the particles that make up the air are close together, the air pressure is high.

When the particles that make up the air are further apart, the air pressure is low.

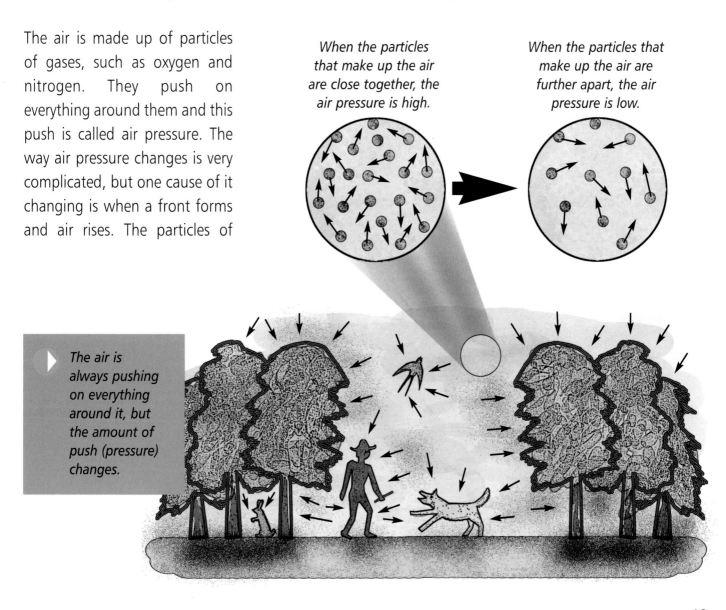

The air is always pushing on everything around it, but the amount of push (pressure) changes.

Air masses and air pressure

Air masses reaching the broad-leaved forests can be made by air from the tropics (the region around the equator) or by air from the polar regions. Air from the tropics sinks and piles up over hot desert land or a warm sea. The air takes up the features of its surroundings and becomes either warm and dry or warm and wet. The heat it receives is not great enough to make it rise very far, and so the air pressure remains high.

Air from the polar regions sinks onto sea or land. It becomes cold and wet if it sinks onto the sea, or cold and dry if it sinks onto land. In either case, the pressure of this air becomes high as it sinks to the Earth's surface.

When air masses meet and a front forms, air rises and this can be detected by a fall in air pressure. After the front has moved away, the rising air is replaced by air that is not rising. This makes the air pressure rise again.

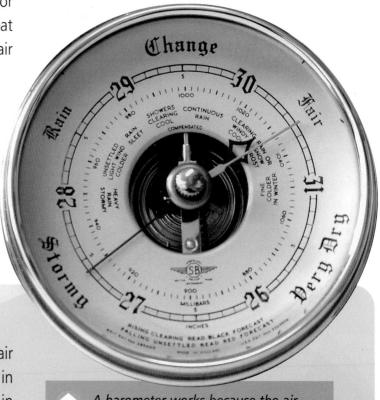

A barometer works because the air outside presses on a metal box inside the instrument. This box contains a vacuum: there is no air inside it.

Measuring air pressure

A barometer is an instrument for measuring air pressure. In the kind of barometer found in homes, there is a metal box. Its sides move in and out, depending on the air pressure, and this change is recorded by a needle on the barometer dial. The movement of the needle is used to predict the weather.

1 If the air pressure is not changing, the weather may remain the same.

2 If the air pressure falls quickly, a front may be coming and rain can be expected.

3 If the air pressure rises, a period of fine weather may soon follow.

Some people who make expeditions into forest regions take a portable barometer, as part of a watch or pocket **altimeter**.

Make a simple barometer

Set up this barometer and look for changes in air pressure.

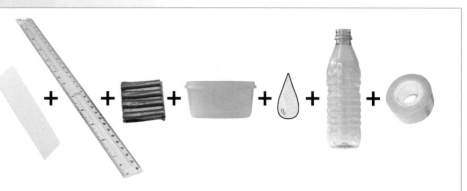

You need a piece of card about 10cm x 3cm, a ruler, a lump of modelling clay about 6cm across, a bowl with sides about 8cm high, water, a plastic bottle, sticky tape.

1 Make a scale on the card by drawing lines 0.5cm apart. Mark the centre line with a dot.

2 Shape the modelling clay into a ring and make four arches in it. Place the ring in the bowl, with the arches facing down, and pour water into the bowl to a depth of about 5cm.

3 Pour water into the bottle until it is about three-quarters full. Then cover the opening of the bottle with your fingers and quickly turn the bottle over and place the opening under the water in the bowl. Rest the opening of the bottle on top of the ring.

4 Tape the scale to the bottle, with the dot against the level of the water.

5 After two hours, see if the water level in the bottle has changed. If it has gone up, the air pressure is rising. If it has gone down, the air pressure is falling.

6 Over the next few days, keep a record of your barometer readings and compare them with the weather. Can you use the barometer to predict the weather?

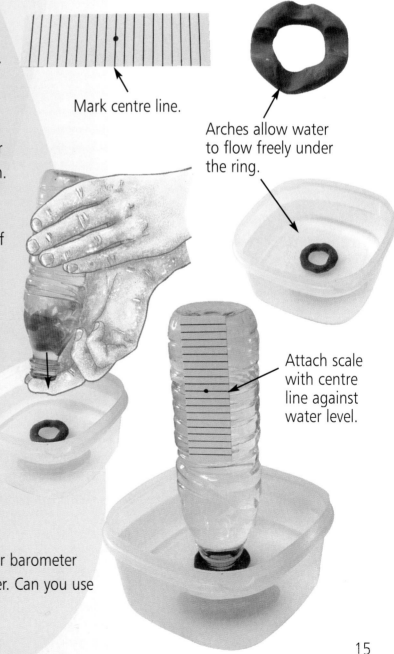

Mark centre line.

Arches allow water to flow freely under the ring.

Attach scale with centre line against water level.

How conifers survive

Plants need water and light, so that they can make food. They also need warmth in order to stay alive. Yet conifers grow on land that is frozen for most of the year, which means they cannot get water. Often when water arrives, it is in the form of snow. This is solid water, but plants can only use liquid water. The summers are short and cool, so the conifers only receive enough light and heat for a small part of the year. How can they survive? Here are some ways in which conifers are **adapted** for survival.

Conical shape directs snow falling on the branches to the ground. This stops snow from building up on the branches and breaking them with its weight.

*Small surface area of needle-like leaves prevents the tree from losing too much water by **transpiration**.*

Waxy coating of leaves keeps surfaces clear, so that any sunlight can reach the food-making parts of the leaves. Also, snow slips off the waxy leaves, so it does not build up on the branches.

Very springy or flexible wood allows the trunk to bend without snapping in the strong winter winds.

Branches can bend easily, without snapping, so snow can slide off.

Dark green leaves absorb (take in) more heat from the Sun's rays. (Paler leaves would reflect more heat.)

The tree stays in leaf all year round, so it is ready to make food whenever there is enough light. Conifers do shed their leaves, but not all at once. They are continually shedding leaves and replacing them. This process is slow and a leaf may live for up to seven years on a tree.

Transpiration

All plants move water through their bodies by allowing water to escape from their leaves as water vapour. This is part of a process called transpiration. As water vapour moves out of the plant through tiny holes in the underside of the leaves, more water is drawn in from the soil by the plant roots.

For much of the year, the frozen ground prevents conifers from collecting water via their roots, and so they must save as much as possible of the water that is in their trunks and branches. Conifer leaves are needle-like so that they have only a small surface through which they can lose water. This slows down the speed at which the leaves lose water and helps conserve water in the tree until the ground thaws out.

▲ *Among the needle-like leaves grow pine cones. This photograph shows female cones.*

Pine cones

Plants use **pollen** in order to breed. In spring and summer, the pollen is spread by insects or by the wind. Conifers use the wind to spread their pollen. If the pollen were carried by insects, there would be less time for it to be spread, because when spring comes in a coniferous forest, the insects need time to warm up and grow into 'flying machines'. The summer is short and the trees do not have time to wait.

In conifers, pollen is produced by male pine cones. It must then reach the seed-making or female cones in order for the conifers to breed. Female cones are much larger than male cones and are the ones that people sometimes collect.

In the cold summers, the breeding processes can only take place slowly, so in the first year the female cone simply collects the pollen. In the second year it makes seeds, and in the third year it releases the seeds.

▲ *These male pine cones are releasing pollen into the wind.*

Predicting the weather with pine cones

Pine cones release their seeds into the air. The seeds have wings, so they can be caught by the wind and spread to help the forest grow. Rain can knock the seeds out of the air and stop them spreading. Pine cones therefore open in dry weather to release their seeds. When wet weather approaches, the air becomes damp. Can pine cones tell the difference between dry and damp air?

You need two plastic jars with lids, water, two pieces of string, two pine cones about the same size, sticky tape, a sunny windowsill.

1 Pour about 1cm of water into one jar.

2 Tie one end of each piece of string to a pine cone. Then lower each pine cone into a jar so that it hangs in the middle of the jar. Tape the string to the outside of the jar to hold the pine cone in place. Put the lids on the jars and place the jars on a sunny windowsill.

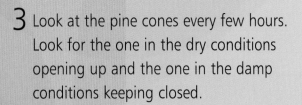

3 Look at the pine cones every few hours. Look for the one in the dry conditions opening up and the one in the damp conditions keeping closed.

4 Swap the pine cones between the jars and see what happens to them.

Some people keep pine cones outside their homes and look at them to tell when dry or wet weather is coming.

How broad-leaved trees survive

Broad-leaved trees like the hickory are *deciduous*: they drop their leaves in autumn.

To the south of the boreal forest and taiga the summers are longer and the winters less cold and dark. Periods of dry weather follow periods of wet weather throughout the year. This means there is a regular supply of water and the trees do not need to conserve water, as the conifer trees further north must do. However, in many places, the ground freezes in winter and this cuts off the supply of water to the roots. Broad-leaved trees are adapted to these conditions in the following ways.

Water control

As there is plenty of water for most of the year, the trees have large leaves with many holes on their undersides, to let large amounts of water vapour escape. This makes a huge water pump to drive the water up from the roots, so the tree can make food.

The large leaves also trap plenty of sunlight and make large amounts of food. However, if the trees kept their leaves in the winter, when the roots cannot get enough water, the tree would lose all the water from inside its trunk, dry out and die. To prevent this happening, most broad-leaved trees are deciduous: this means they let their leaves fall in the autumn. This greatly reduces the amount of water lost by the tree and therefore it can survive through the winter. The next spring the tree grows new leaves.

Seeds and fruits

Broad-leaved trees have flowers. They may be small and grouped together into catkins, as in hazel or hickory. These flowers produce pollen and are called male flowers. The pollen is released into the wind. Smaller, female flowers on the trees receive the pollen and make seeds.

The flowers of some trees, like the horse chestnut, have large petals to attract insects. The insects carry the pollen from flower to flower.

When a flower receives pollen from another flower, it makes seeds inside fruits, which ripen in the autumn. The purpose of the fruits is to spread out the seeds, so that new plants can grow without being tangled up with each other. Some fruits are juicy and colourful, to attract animals to eat them. If the seeds inside the fruit are eaten, they pass through the digestive system of the animals and fall to the ground unharmed.

Horse chestnut flowers attract insects to spread their pollen.

Some seeds are spread by squirrels when they collect and bury nuts for the winter.

Some fruits become woody and we call them nuts. Animals, such as squirrels, collect and store nuts in various places in the forest. Over the winter, they eat some of the nuts but forget about others. These forgotten nuts may produce new tree seedlings in the following year.

Many trees such as the maple and the ash have winged fruits. The wings slow the speed of the falling fruit and increase its chance of being carried away by the wind.

Testing winged fruit

The wings on a fruit, like the maple fruits in this photograph, can make it spin and slow its fall through the air. If the seed can fall slowly, it has a greater chance of being carried by the wind to a place where it may grow into a new tree. Compare the way two model winged fruits spin. Which is more likely to be carried away by the wind?

You need paper, pencil, ruler, scissors, two paper-clips.

1 Draw two shapes on the paper as shown below.

2 Cut out the shapes along lines A-B, B-C, C-D and D-A.

3 Cut along lines W-X and Y-Z.

4 Fold along the dotted lines to make each shape into a model winged fruit. Then fit a paper-clip to the bottom.

5 Hold up each model fruit in turn and let it go. Which is the better spinner?

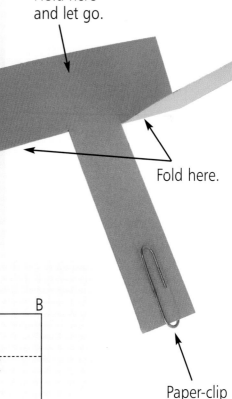

Hold here and let go.

Fold here.

Paper-clip fits here.

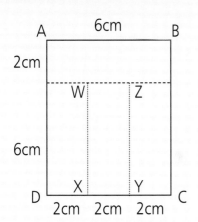

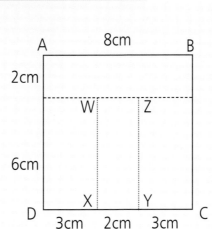

Why leaves fall in autumn

The veins in a leaf are two kinds of tube. One kind brings water into the leaf from the twig, and the other kind takes food from the leaf to the rest of the tree. In autumn, broad-leaved trees block these tubes with a corky substance between the twig and leaf stalk. The leaves then dry out and fall, leaving scars on the twig and the corky plugs stopping any more water escaping.

Buds ready for the new year

As a twig grows, it forms buds on its sides called **lateral buds**. Inside each bud is a tiny stem and curled-up leaves. The buds at the end of a twig are larger than the rest and are called **terminal buds**. They contain a cluster of tiny flowers. The contents of all the buds are covered with tough scales, which protect them from the harsh winter.

In spring the tree takes up water from the soil and passes it to the buds. The scales fall away and the water makes the stems and leaves unfold. As sunlight falls on the leaves, they use some of the water to make food for growth. The food provides materials and energy for the leaves and stems to grow and the flowers to form fully and produce pollen.

The growing twig

During spring and summer, food is used to make the twig grow longer and push out its leaves towards the light. If the terminal bud is not damaged, the lateral buds do not open. All the food made in the leaves is used to make the twig longer and push the leaves further from the tree so that they are not shaded by branches above. If the terminal bud is damaged, the lateral buds open and produce side shoots.

Lateral buds do not open unless the terminal bud is damaged.

A deer nibbling on a tree may damage a terminal bud.

Comparing the growth of twigs

When the bud scales fall away, they leave a scar. The scales around the terminal bud make a ring scar all around the twig. This is called an age ring. You can find out how much a twig has grown in a year by measuring the distance between two age rings.

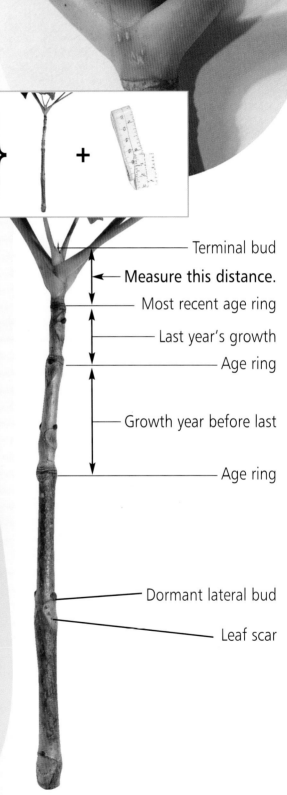

You need twigs of horse chestnut, oak, ash and any other tree that grows locally, a tape measure.

Horse chestnut *Oak* *Ash* +

1 Look at the photograph on the right and learn how to identify age rings.

2 Take one of the twigs and find its terminal bud and the most recent age ring.

3 Measure the distance between the age ring and the bud and record it.

4 Repeat steps 2 and 3 with each of the other twigs.

5 Which twig grew the most in the year and which grew the least?

6 If you can examine a large twig, you should be able to find another two or three age rings along it. Measure the distances between the age rings and record the growth for the last few years. Did the twig always grow the same amount each year?

7 When a tree is surviving well, its twigs grow long. When it is more difficult to survive, the twigs grow less well. What did the age rings on a twig tell you about how the tree has survived in the last few years?

Terminal bud
Measure this distance.
Most recent age ring
Last year's growth
Age ring

Growth year before last

Age ring

Dormant lateral bud

Leaf scar

Clothes for the forest

People like the Sami who live in the forest today sometimes wear traditional clothing made from animal skin.

Most people who live in the forest today wear modern clothes. In the past, all people living in the forest made their clothes from the materials around them.

Using forest materials

When animals were killed for food, their skins were removed and made into clothes. First the skins were cleaned of their flesh with stone scrapers. Hair in an animal skin is of different lengths, and the longer hairs were combed out with combs made of wood or bone. This made the skins smoother. Then the skins were hung up over a smoky fire, so that substances in the smoke settled on the skins. These substances stopped **microbes** such as **bacteria** from rotting the skins, and also helped to keep them soft and flexible, so they were comfortable to wear.

The skins were cut with stone knives, and needles of bone or stone were used to make holes so that the skins could be sewn together. Another material from animals was used to sew the skin. This material is called sinew and it comes from the tendons that hold the muscles to bones. Sheets of sinew were torn into strips and rolled to make very strong threads to hold the pieces of skin together.

Clothes to match the weather

As the weather changed during the year, the forest and woodland people changed their dress to remain comfortable. In wet weather, in the northwest of North America, people wore rain hats made of wooden sticks woven together. Capes made from bark also kept the body dry. Thick bark was stripped from a tree, using a knife. This allowed some bark to remain so the tree could survive. The pieces of bark were stitched together with twine to make the cape.

In some parts of North America in summer, the men wore breechcloths and kilts and the women wore skirts and leggings. (A breechcloth was a piece of cloth worn between the legs and fastened to a belt at the front and back.) In winter the men also wore shirts and the women wore full-length dresses. All these garments were made of deerskin. When it was very cold, robes made of beaver fur or swan or turkey feathers were worn on top of the other clothes.

Layers of clothes

In many forest regions the weather changes not just during the year, but during the day. The morning may be dry and warm and the afternoon cold and wet. People trekking through woods and forests must take clothes with them so they can stay comfortable in all weathers. They do not need to wear all the clothes all the time, but keep some in a bag carried on their back. When conditions are warm or dry, they can remove some layers. When the weather becomes cold or wet, they can add some layers.

Hat prevents loss of heat from the head in cold weather.

Windproof and rainproof jacket.

Gloves for frosty mornings and cold winter weather.

Pullover made of wool to provide extra warmth.

Loose-fitting shirt to allow sweat to escape into the air.

Cotton vest soaks up sweat from skin and passes it through to shirt.

Cotton underpants. In cold weather, long johns can be worn over them.

▶ These are the clothes you should wear, or carry with you, if you are trekking through the forest.

Waterproof over-trousers to wear in heavy rain.

Trousers made from quick-drying material that is not easily torn.

Can natural materials keep in warmth?

If someone is caught out in the forest when the weather becomes very cold, they may not have enough layers of clothing to keep them warm. Could natural materials like dry grass or leaves help? Use this fair test to find out.

You need some dry grass or dry leaves, two pieces of the same cloth, two plastic cups, warm water at about 40°C, a thermometer, a clock. Ask an adult to help you with the warm water.

1 Wrap one piece of cloth loosely round the dry grass or leaves. Then put a plastic cup in the middle of the dry material.

2 Wrap the other piece of cloth round the other plastic cup.

3 Pour warm water into each cup. Make sure that each is filled to the same level.

4 Take the temperature of the water in each cup and write it down.

5 Repeat step 4 every two minutes for 30 minutes.

6 Look at the results and see if the water in the cup surrounded by the grass or leaves cooled down more slowly than the water in the other cup. If it did, these natural materials have useful insulating properties.

Material wrapped around dry grass

Check temperature every two minutes.

Shelter

This is a reconstruction of a Native American settlement, in Jamestown, Virginia.

People who lived in woods and forests used the natural materials around them to make their homes.

Wigwams

The most famous woodland home is the wigwam of North America. It was made by bending poles into large arches, to form a dome-shaped framework. This was covered with slabs of bark from the birch or the elm. Once the wigwam was made, it could not be easily dismantled and moved.

People who wanted to move around in the forest, perhaps to follow the herds of deer for food, made cone-shaped wigwams. The poles for the framework were simply propped together and tied at the top with rope made from plant fibres. Bark was then laid on the framework. In the Russian forests today, the Evenk people make conical homes covered in cloth.

People often think that wigwams and teepees are the same thing, but they are not. Teepees are conical tents covered in buffalo skins.

Longhouses

In the forests of northwest North America, people built longhouses out of poles covered with elm bark. These houses were so large that a few families could live inside one. Each family had part of the house partitioned off from the others for privacy.

Finding shelter

Sometimes people trekking through a wood or forest may need to shelter and rest overnight. On a rocky hill or mountainside, they may find a cave. This may look a good place to shelter, but in some countries it might also be the home of a bear!

A good place to make a shelter could be where a low bough of a conifer sweeps close to the ground. Other branches can be cut off and leant against the bough to make a place to sleep.

Fallen branches could also be placed against one side of a log and covered with **turf** to make a shelter for the night.

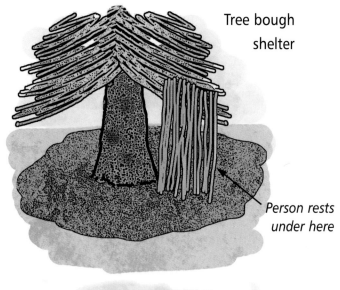

Tree bough shelter

Person rests under here

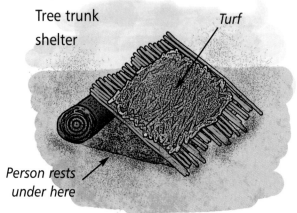

Tree trunk shelter

Turf

Person rests under here

Tents

Many trekkers carry their shelter with them – a tent. A tent is composed of a fly-sheet and an inner tent. This allows the campers to keep dry. Inside the tent, the campers give off water vapour in their breath. The inner tent is made of a material that lets this vapour pass through it easily. The fly-sheet is made of waterproof material, which helps to keep the inner tent dry. The water vapour may pass under the fly-sheet out into the air or it may condense on the inside of the fly-sheet. There must be a gap between the fly-sheet and the inner tent. If they were to touch, droplets of water could pass back into the inner tent. The inner tent and fly-sheet are kept pulled tight by guy-ropes, so that they do not touch.

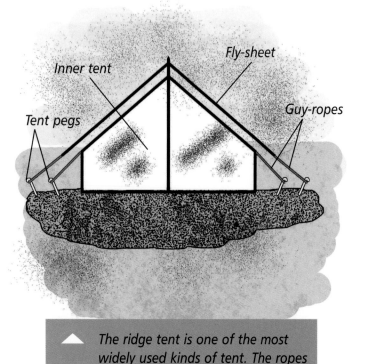

Fly-sheet

Inner tent

Guy-ropes

Tent pegs

▲ *The ridge tent is one of the most widely used kinds of tent. The ropes are held in place by tent pegs.*

Why should you knock a tent peg right into the ground?

Tent pegs must prevent the tent from being blown away and stand up to a pulling force from the guy-ropes. Campers are advised to knock in the tent pegs so that only the tops remain above ground. How does the depth of the peg in the ground affect the force it can take without moving? Use a force meter to find out.

You need access to a lawn, a tent peg, a force meter measuring up to 10 **newtons** (N).

1 Put in the tent peg at 45°, but only push it in about a third of its length.

2 Hook the force meter to the top of the tent peg and pull steadily. Record the strength of the force at which the tent peg is pulled into a vertical position.

3 Repeat steps 1 and 2, but with the tent peg pushed in to about two-thirds its length.

4 Repeat steps 1 and 2, but with the tent peg pushed in to its full length so that only the hook or ring remains above ground.

5 Which position needed the most force to move the tent peg?

6 Which position needed the least force to move the tent peg?

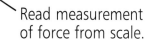

Pull here.

Read measurement of force from scale.

Travelling through the woods

People who lived in the forests and woods travelled about to find food. Sometimes they moved camp to a place where more food could be found. When they moved, they took baskets of food, and utensils like wooden spoons and dishes, with them. They also took their animal-skin clothes, but they left behind the wood and bark that made their homes. These materials would be available at the next campsite.

In North America, many people simply walked through the woods to the next camp. When women took their babies on journeys through the woods, they carried them on their back, on a papoose board. The baby was wrapped in furs packed with dry moss, for warmth, and then fastened to the board.

In Russia and parts of Europe, people used reindeer to carry their belongings, including babies.

Canoe trips

There are many rivers and lakes in the forests and woods of North America. They were used for travel,

The Evenk people of Russia still herd reindeer in the forests. When the reindeer have eaten most of the leaves in a particular place, the Evenk move on to another part of the forest. They pack their belongings on some of the reindeer and ride others along pathways between the trees.

as roads are used today. The main kind of boat, which was used both for travel and for fishing, was the birch-bark canoe. Strips of white cedar were made into a frame. Then pieces of birch bark were tied securely to the frame with roots. The canoe was made watertight by coating the bark with black spruce **resin**, a waxy substance made by black spruce trees.

Carrying a load

Most modern trekkers carry their equipment in a backpack. Everything they need is packed in, in the order in which it will be needed. At the top, so that they can be first out, are the water bottles and first aid kit. Below them is the food, and below the food are the tent and sleeping bag. At the end of a tiring day, the food can be taken out and cooking

begun, and the tent can be set up by the time the meal is ready.

People must take care when they carry any kind of load, so that they do not injure themselves. Wearing a backpack or any pack correctly is important. If the pack is just strapped to the shoulders, the trekker has to lean forwards to keep his or her balance. This makes some muscles ache and can damage the spinal column. If the pack is set up correctly, with a belt around the hips, the trekker can walk upright comfortably and safely.

Weight

Weight

If a heavy backpack is just strapped to the shoulders, most of its weight passes through the spinal column and can cause injuries. But with a hip belt, three-quarters of the pack's weight passes safely through the hips and down the legs.

Finding directions

You should have a compass, to check the direction in which you are walking. You might also know how to tell directions by noticing the time and the position of the Sun and shadows. But, even if the clouds are so low that the Sun cannot be seen, it is still possible to find directions.

Trees and the Sun

A tree growing on its own will grow towards the strength of the sunlight. The branches on the sunniest side will be horizontal, while those on the opposite side will point more vertically. In the Northern Hemisphere, the horizontal branches point south. In the Southern Hemisphere, the horizontal branches point north.

Even a tree stump can show the way. The rings on the sunniest side will be thicker than the rings on

Tree branches grow towards the Sun. If this tree is in the Northern Hemisphere, its horizontal branches are pointing south.

the opposite side. This is because the warmth from the sunshine makes the wood of a tree grow more than on the cooler, shadier side.

The moss on a tree trunk can also help you find directions. It is bright green on the sunny side and more brown and yellow on the opposite side. The moss on the sunny side is greener because the sunlight makes it produce more green **pigment** or colouring to help it make food.

Trees and the wind

In many places, the wind blows from the same direction for most of the year. This wind is called the prevailing wind. It blows the trees as they grow and makes them bend permanently. They bend away from the wind. If you know the direction of the prevailing wind, the trees can show you where it is.

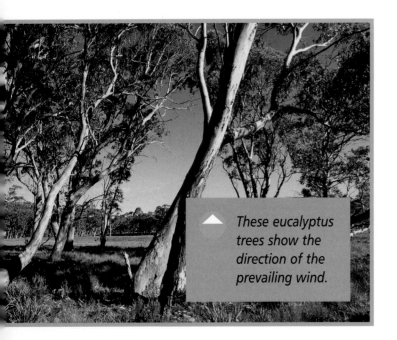

These eucalyptus trees show the direction of the prevailing wind.

Foods from the forest

People who lived in the forests looked for food to help them survive in every season of the year.

Spring

In the spring, deciduous trees draw up water to make their buds burst and leaves grow. The food stored in the wood (see page 9) is turned into sugar to provide energy for the buds and leaves, and this sugar is added to the water as it rises through the tree. The water in a tree, with substances dissolved in it, is called sap.

The maple tree produces a large amount of sugar and makes a sweet-tasting sap. In North America people collected this sap by cutting a notch in the tree trunk and letting the sap run into a cup. The sap was then heated and turned into maple syrup – a high-energy food that could be used all year.

Many plants, such as the burdock, store another high-energy food called **starch** in their roots. They use this to make new shoots in the spring. In the past, people used digging sticks to dig up the roots and then boiled them to make a meal. They also boiled and ate young shoots of plants such as nettles. The young leaves of trees such as the beech and hawthorn were eaten raw.

 Metal buckets are attached to maple trees to collect the sap to produce maple syrup.

Summer

People did not kill many animals in the spring, when they were breeding. They left them alone to increase their numbers and provide more food for other times of year. In the summer, people began to hunt and fish again.

In forests with hot, dry summers, the meat and fish could be set out in the Sun to dry. Once the food was dried, it could be stored for use when the weather was too bad to hunt or fish. If the food had not been dried, it would have been attacked by **moulds** and bacteria and rotted away. But without water on the surface of the food, these microbes cannot live or breed.

In forests with damp summers, the meat and fish were set up in a smoke house. Smoke dries food and coats it in chemicals that stop microbes attacking it.

Berries and mushrooms appear on the forest floor in autumn. Forest people learned which were safe to eat. But you should never eat any fungi or plants that you find in the wild, as they could be poisonous.

Autumn

In autumn people gathered fruits such as blackberries. They also collected nuts and ground them into flour. In oak woodlands in California, acorns were collected and washed, to remove their bitter taste, then ground up to make flour. The flour was used to make porridge and cakes.

Large numbers of **fungi** produce their mushroom-like **fruiting bodies** in the autumn. Some fungi are edible and have been used as food, while others are deadly poisonous. It takes great skill to tell edible fungi from poisonous ones and you should never eat or even touch any fungi that you see growing in the wild.

Winter

In winter, some fruits that develop late in the year, such as the rosehip, were collected for food. Usually, food that had been gathered and stored in other seasons was used until the spring weather returned.

Food for the trek

People on a trek or expedition take food with them. They could not afford the time it would take to gather foods from the forest. Also, if all the people who visit forests were to collect food there, the forest life could be permanently damaged.

Much of our food contains water, and water makes food heavy. The food that is carried in a backpack is dry food, so that it is light in weight. Some foods, called dehydrated foods, have had the water taken away from them. This makes them smaller in size and lighter in weight and ideal for taking on a trek. Water is added to make the food into a meal.

On a trek, breakfast might be oats or dried fruits, which contain plenty of energy, vitamins and fibre. During the day, when people stop to rest, they may eat chocolate bars or biscuits, to give them energy to keep walking. A main meal is usually made in the evening. Lentils and beans must be soaked in water to soften them before cooking. They provide protein. Rice can be placed in water and then boiled. This provides energy.

This trekker is preparing a meal using dehydrated fruits and vegetables.

A healthy diet

A diet is the food that a person usually eats in the course of a day, week or month. A healthy diet is one that provides:

1 energy for moving and for warmth;

2 protein for growth and for the repair of cuts and bruises;

3 vitamins and **minerals**, which keep many parts of the body such as the skin and bones healthy; and

4 fibre which helps the food pass along the digestive system.

Does food need to be kept dry?

Dry food is carried on many treks because it is light in weight. It should always be kept in watertight containers. But what would happen if some water mixed with it while it was stored in a backpack or at camp? Try this fair test to find out.

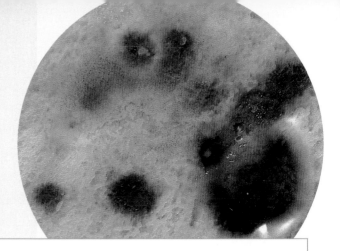

You need two plastic bags which can be sealed (e.g. ziplock), two slices of bread, an eye dropper, water, a warm place such as an airing cupboard.

1 Put one slice of bread in a bag and seal the bag.

2 Have the second bag ready for the second slice of bread. Fill the eye dropper with water and put ten drops of water on this slice. Then slide it into the bag and seal the bag.

First piece of bread sealed in bag

3 Put both bags in a warm place and look at the slices every day, without opening the bags.

4 At some point you should see mould growing on the bread. Which slice grows the mould? How many days does it take to for the mould to appear?

Place ten drops of water on the second slice and seal it in the second bag.

5 Let an adult get rid of the unopened bags for you.

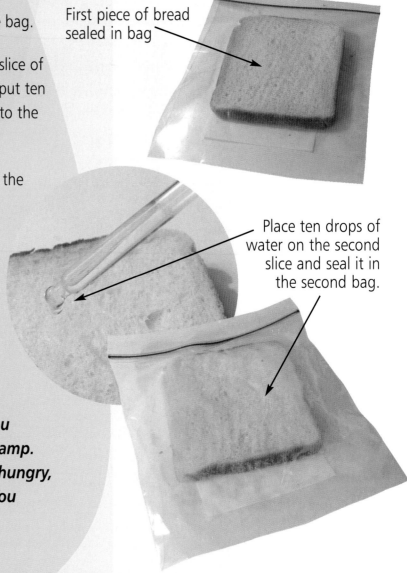

Mould makes food inedible. Imagine if you were careless and let your dry food get damp. You might come back to camp, tired and hungry, to find that the food had gone mouldy. You would have to make a new trek to find something to eat.

Drinking water

At the start of an expedition, everyone fills their water bottles from a tap. After this water has been used, they must take care that any other water they drink does not contain harmful germs.

Water containers

There are a wide range of water containers that trekkers can use. Some prefer plastic bottles, but they must be careful to keep them away from campfires. Others prefer steel containers, because they are easier to clean than plastic ones. But steel is heavy. Some plastic water bags can be folded up and packed away when they are not needed.

Water sources

There are usually plenty of streams, rivers and lakes in forest regions. The water may look pure, but further along you may find a dead animal such as a deer in the water. All water needs to be treated, to destroy any bacteria it may contain and make it safe to drink. Many people prefer to treat water by boiling it, but another method is to add chemicals, called chlorine and iodine, to the water. Great care must be taken with these chemicals, because they are not suitable for everyone, such as people who are **allergic** to iodine. Also, the amount of chemicals added to the water must be carefully measured to make sure that all the germs are killed. Water that has been treated with chemicals can have an unpleasant taste. This can be covered by adding a fruit-flavoured drink mix.

In forests on mountains, streams and rivers form rushing waterfalls.

Fire

Before making a campfire, it is very important to clear the ground so that there is nothing nearby that could catch fire.

When trekkers make a camp, they like to light a campfire. This provides heat for boiling water, cooking food, drying clothes and keeping people warm. It is very important that the fire is controlled, to avoid the danger of setting the wood or forest on fire.

The fire should be made in the centre of a large clearing, where there are no branches reaching overhead. The turf should be dug out and the fire set up on bare soil.

The 'triangle of fire'

A fire needs fuel, oxygen and heat. These can be thought of as the 'triangle of fire', to help people remember how to start a fire and how to put it out.

Making heat

In Stone Age times, **flint** and a **mineral** called iron pyrites were used to make heat. A piece of flint was held in one hand and struck against a piece of iron pyrites held in the other hand. This produces sparks, which can provide heat to start a fire.

Later, when people had learnt how to make iron and steel, flint and steel were used to make sparks. Flint and steel are still used today by some trekkers, but many people now use matches.

Fuel for the fire

The forest provides the fuel. This must be dry. Since the source of heat, such as a spark or match flame, is small, the first fuel to be set burning must also be small. This first fuel is called **tinder**. Dry grass is a common tinder.

The next fuel, which is set burning by the tinder, is called kindling. This is made of small, thin twigs. Once the kindling has begun to burn, larger pieces of fuel, such as small branches and small logs, can be added to the fire.

Flint

Iron pyrites

Oxygen

The air supplies the oxygen that the fire needs. Care must be taken when building the fire that the air can reach all the fuel. If the fuel is packed too tightly together, there will not be enough air to get it burning.

Putting out the fire

The fire should be allowed to die down by not placing any more fuel on it. The **embers** should be spread out so that they can lose heat, and then water should be poured over them, to cool them further. The water should also pass into the soil where it can cool down any roots there so that they do not start to burn when the campers have gone. Finally the cold embers should be scattered, and the turf that was dug out should be replaced.

Tinder

Kindling

Logs

Forest wildlife

This red-headed woodpecker is flying towards its nest hole in a forest tree.

Koalas feed on eucalpytus trees in the Australian forests. Their toes are adapted for climbing.

The trees provide a sheltered place for many plants and animals to live. Winds roaring on the edges of the forest are stopped from passing through it by the trunks and branches. Inside, the air is still and safe for insects to fly about. The air trapped in the forest helps to keep the forest a little warmer than outside, so deer and wild boar take shelter there in cold winter weather.

Home for plants

In deciduous woods, the leaves shade the ground in summer and make it difficult for smaller plants to grow there. However, the small plants have developed a way of surviving by sending up their leaves and flowers early in the year to catch the Sun's light and warmth before the trees burst into leaf.

Home for animals

The trees are home to many animals. Caterpillars feed on their leaves and small birds feed on the caterpillars. Beetles live in the bark and woodpeckers drill into the tree trunks to feed on the beetles.

Each animal has developed in some way to survive there. Caterpillars have legs that allow them to grip the leaves, and jaws that allow them to bite along the leaf edges. Small birds have feet that grip the twigs and branches and prevent them from falling off. The woodpecker has a beak like a chisel for cutting its way into the bark.

Testing birds' feet

Most birds have three toes pointing forwards and one toe, the hind toe, pointing back. In some birds the hind toe is short, in others it is longer. Which type of hind toe do you think a bird perching on a tree has?

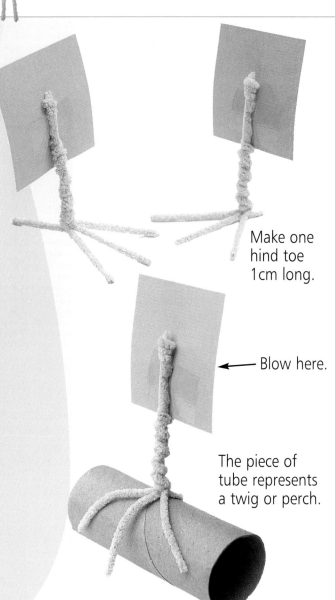

You need 12 pipe-cleaners, 3 pieces of paper 7cm square, sticky tape, a wooden rod or piece of cardboard tube about 4cm in diameter.

1 Twist four pipe-cleaners together to make a bird's foot, as the photos show. The forward-pointing toes should be 5cm long and the hind toe should be 1cm long.

2 Repeat step 1 but make the hind toe 2.5cm long.

3 Repeat step 1 but make the hind toe 5cm long.

4 Attach a square of paper to the first foot with sticky tape and set up the foot on the perch.

5 Blow on the paper and note what happens to the foot.

6 Repeat steps 4 and 5 with the second foot.

7 Repeat steps 4 and 5 with the third foot.

8 What kind of foot do you think small woodland birds have?

Make one hind toe 1cm long.

← Blow here.

The piece of tube represents a twig or perch.

41

Animals to avoid

In most woods and forests you need to beware of bees and wasps. You may need to look out for poisonous snakes, and in a very few forests, there is danger from bears.

Bees and wasps

These insects make nests, which they will defend if anyone comes near them. Bees and wasps have stings, which they inject into the skin of someone who comes too close. This may cause a painful swelling, because the sting contains a poison. In some people, a bee or wasp sting can cause an **allergic shock**, which can be fatal. Bees' and wasps' nests should simply be left alone.

Snakes

In North America you may find rattlesnakes and copper-headed snakes. In Australia there are many poisonous snakes, such as the brown snake. In Europe, the adder lives in open country with few trees, but can also be found in sunny clearings in woods. When a snake is seen, it should be left alone and given a chance to move away.

Bears

When travelling through forests where bears live, some people tie a bell to their backpack so that it rings as they move along. Other people shout or sing. The sounds usually drive the bears away. When a camp is made, bears may be attracted to it by the smell of food. Food should be stored at least 100 metres from the camp. If it is slung from a tree with rope, so that it is 4 metres above the ground and just over 3 metres from the trunk, then a bear cannot reach it.

Black bears live in the broad-leaved forests of the eastern United States. Trekkers in these forests must take precautions to keep them away.

How fast can you join different kinds of rope?

Ropes can be used for many things for survival. In the forest they may be used to make a rope ladder, set up a hammock, bind branches together to make a shelter, or even make a guide rope that can be used at night to direct campers from their tent to the outside toilet called the latrine. Speed can be important in tying ropes – for example, if you are trying to make a shelter in a storm. Sometimes a long rope is needed and only two short ropes can be found. A sheet bend knot is one that can be tied to join two ropes of different thicknesses. How fast can you tie it?

You need a piece of thick string about 20cm long, a piece of thin string about 20cm long, a stopwatch. (Alternatively, you could use two lengths of rope of different thicknesses.)

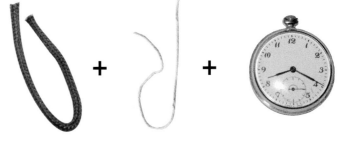

1 Take the string or rope and use the pictures to make a sheet bend knot.

2 Once you have learnt how to make the knot, how fast can you tie it?

3 Sometimes it is dark when people make a camp and need ropes. Can you tie the knot when the room is dark or with your eyes closed?

4 Do different people perform at different speeds when they make a knot? Ask some of your friends to try tying the knot and time them.

This part goes under itself and then over the large string.

Time yourself and your friends.

Rescue

You cannot see very far around you in a forest, so you may sometimes lose sight of your companions. Trekkers often use whistles to signal to each other.

When people set off on an expedition, they should let their family or friends know where they are going and when they will return. Then, if something goes wrong and they don't come back when expected, a rescue party can be sent out.

Searches may be made by aeroplane, but they will also be made on land. All the trees make it difficult to see people in the forests, so signals using light are not useful. Sound can travel through the forest better than light, so all trekkers are advised to take a whistle with them. They can blow the whistle to attract attention and get help.

There is an international code for whistle blasts, which is understood by rangers and rescuers in the forests of many countries. If you blow three short blasts, then three long ones, then three short blasts again, you have given the SOS signal, which means that you are in some kind of distress. You should keep repeating the message, but wait one minute after each time.

If you blow six blasts quickly, one after the other, it means you need help. Again, you should keep repeating the message, at one-minute intervals. Repeating the message helps rescuers to tell where the sound is coming from, so they can move their search closer to you.

When a rescuer hears your whistle, he or she may send back a message of three quick blasts, repeated every minute. This means that your message has been understood.

Sending a message by sound

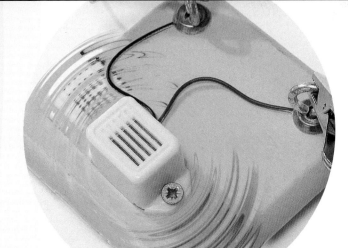

Imagine that you are lost in the forest and have lost your whistle. You have some electrical equipment. See if you can assemble the equipment and send the messages described on page 44.

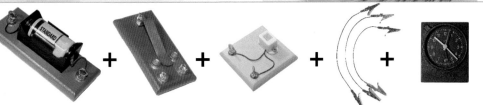

You need a 1.5V battery, a switch, a buzzer, three wires, a clock.

1 Make a circuit as shown in the photograph.

2 Make the SOS signal every minute for five minutes.

3 Make the 'Help needed' signal every minute for five minutes.

4 Make the 'Message understood' signal every minute for five minutes.

5 You could also try making a horn for the buzzer, out of card, and test to see if it makes the sound louder.

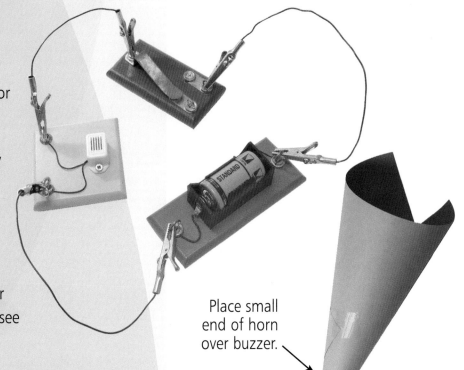

Place small end of horn over buzzer.

The end of the journey

When people reach the end of a journey, they usually feel they have learnt a lot along the way. How did you get on in the forest? What is a deciduous tree? Can you use a pine cone to help you predict the weather? Where would you put your food to stop bears stealing it? Also, on the journey, you have had many chances to try out your science skills of observing, predicting and experimenting. What did you discover? Many people live in areas where forests used to be. Perhaps you are one of them. Outside you may see some trees planted in gardens and parks, but imagine what the view would have looked like when the place was still a forest.

Glossary

adapted   with body features that make it easy to survive in certain places.

allergic   sensitive to a substance. The body reacts to it as if it is harmful.

allergic shock   a reaction of the body to substances in wasp and bee stings and also in nuts and seafood. It can take the form of itching and wheezing and, in extreme cases, the heart may stop.

altimeter   an instrument which measures height above sea level.

bacteria   microscopic living things which feed on dead plants and animals and some materials. Some kinds of bacteria invade other living things to feed and breed and may cause disease.

barometer   an instrument which measures the pressure of the air in the atmosphere. It is used in weather forecasting.

boreal   describes northern regions just outside the Arctic region.

broad-leaved trees   trees with wide, flat leaves. They may be evergreen or deciduous.

chlorophyll   the green pigment in plants which is used for trapping some of the energy in sunlight to make food.

condense   change from a gas to a liquid.

coniferous   describes a wood or forest of conifers.

conifers   types of trees, which have dark, waxy, usually needle-like leaves and which grow cones to help them reproduce.

deciduous   losing leaves at one time of the year and growing new ones later.

embers   pieces of glowing wood. They are burning, but not in flame.

fibre   a thread of a material. Fibre is also a substance in food which is not digested but helps the digestive system to move the food along inside the body.

flint   a piece of rock which is grey or black with a white coating. It is made almost purely from a substance called silica.

fruiting body   the part of a fungus which grows above ground and produces spores such as a toadstool or mushroom.

fungi   a group of organisms which appear to grow like plants, but do not make their own food. They feed on material from the bodies of dead animals and plants.

herbaceous   describes plants that produce new shoots of leaves and flowers each spring and summer, which die back in autumn.

insulating   stopping the movement of heat, or stopping the movement of electricity.

lateral buds	buds that grow from the side of a stem or twig.
marsupial	a type of mammal whose female has a pouch used for rearing its babies.
microbes	tiny forms of life that can only be seen with a powerful microscope.
mineral	a substance in food, needed for good health. Also, a hard glassy, metallic or colourful rocky substance found in the Earth's crust among rocks.
moulds	fungi with bodies that form a hairy coating on the material they feed on.
Neanderthals	a type of human, living from 250,000 years ago until 30,000 years ago.
newtons	units for measuring the size of a force. They are named after the scientist Sir Isaac Newton.
observation	looking at the way something is, or the way in which something happens.
oxygen	a gas found in air and dissolved in water, which is used by nearly all living things to help keep them alive.
pigment	a substance which gives colour to the body of a human, animal or plant.
pollen	tiny grains produced in flowers to help plants reproduce.

protein	a substance in many foods, used by the body for growth and repair of injuries.
resin	a sticky substance made by conifers when their bark is damaged. It prevents insect attack.
starch	a substance made by plants, which is a store of energy. It forms part of our diet.
temperate	describes the region of the Earth between the hot tropical region and the cold regions of the poles.
terminal bud	the bud at the end of a shoot or twig.
tinder	any kind of dry material, such as grass, which can be used to start a fire.
transpiration	a process in which water is lost by evaporation from surfaces of a plant shoot, such as those of the leaves.
tropical	describes the region between the Tropics of Cancer and Capricorn (see pages 6-7). It is usually hot here.
turf	a layer of grass cut from the ground, with soil attached to its roots.
vitamins	substances in food which keep the body in good health.
water vapour	the gas which water forms when it evaporates.

Index